Graduation & Senior Trip
Don't Drint the Water at the Back of the Bus

Southern Short Story Series, 2

DR. TED ARY

Copyright © 2024 Ted Ary
All cover art copyright © 2024 Ted Ary
All Rights Reserved

This is a work of fiction. Names, places, characters and incidents are either the product of the author's imagination or are used fictitiously, and any resemblance to any actual persons, living or dead, businesses, organizations, events or locales is entirely coincidental.

No part of this book may be reproduced or transmitted in any form or by any means, electronic or mechanical, including photocopying, recording, or by any information storage and retrieval system, without permission in writing from the author.

Publishing Coordinator – Sharon Kizziah-Holmes

Paperback-Press
an imprint of A & S Publishing
Paperback Press, LLC.
Springfield, Missouri

ISBN -13: 978-1-964559-38-4

In Memory of Jeff Hunter
Moultrie High School
Class of 1970

THE STORY

No one knew from whence it came. In retrospect, fifty years later, it was one of those known facts with no beginning or end. Some postulated that the thought had been contrived at some meeting where ideas are tossed out like bread crumbs to mice. Maybe, as a lame suggestion or an idle comment, an idea so outrageous, that some suggested that it was in some group where ideas are shouted over each other in an attempt at creativity. The loudest and most boisterous wins. Then, everybody glares at the victor.

Nonetheless, it was disseminated widely and rapidly. It involved the destination of the Class of 1971, the senior class trip. Entire crowds of students launched into rhetoric between classes. It was a rumor first, then a fact, then a fantasy, then back to some nebulous merger of both. The masses kept it moving. It raced around the high school like a flame on a dry hay field off Highway 37. Tongues wagged. Ears burned. Guts churned. Couples yearned. The Senior Class Trip of 1971 was to be consummated, as one might say, in Nassau, Bahamas. This would be out of the country from man and beast and far from the laws of the United States of America and even further from parental guidance. Mom and Dad certain to be, at least for a few days, absent from memory and devoid of governing outcomes, incomes and outflows.

Of course, it had never been done. No sanctioned high school trip by the Board of Education or the hierarchy of prune faced educators in Moultrie, Ga. had ever suggested that the real world should be discovered at the risk of the Board losing face with the public. There could be accidents, mayhem and madness, for sure. Perhaps it could be considered just a jaunt, a private trip, a little junket of sorts to gleam a little sun, sand, and tan. What could be wrong with such a benign endeavor? The sun did shine on both South Georgia and the Bahamas, and would do so regardless of who was where. The sun was inevitable. The group would merely be under the same sun that they had left in South Georgia.

It is all in the way a topic is framed. But, who could frame it? These were grown people anyway. They were 18 - legal age. Well, not exactly. Drinking was age 21, Getting drafted was age 18, driving was age 16, naked movies viewed on a hotel TV were age 21. So technically, they could drive and fight, but could not drink and watch. The Class of 71 could enter a bar in Hanoi in battle, but technically could not order a rum and coke. The age of assumed innocence was, at least for now, still abiding in the Senior Class. But, would that innocence and purity be marred, scarred and shamefully broadcast to God and everybody with wagging tongues, upon a return to peaceful Moultrie, Ga from an island.

In their defense, they were to be high school graduates. Bonafide. Solidified. They had worked hard, most of them, and had achieved great status both in science and muscle. After graduation night, they were not a group, of any type, with connection to the school system. They were reduced to a framed picture of a diploma hung on a prominent living room wall. Relatives and parents would fawn over the adage about 'how time had flown." They were each floundering or stable, in the nebulous world of adulthood, all rights and privileges thereof. Some were certainly walking on more solid ground than others. Others were in quicksand before even departing the United States. However, in some category of worldly fashion, some third world or advanced country designations, they had achieved, with that square hard diploma, grown up status. They were full bred, full blown and full throttle ready to burst into real life with no boundaries or limits. The world by the tale comes to mind.

And, who could blame the Board of Education? This would be a private endeavor with permission freely given by the parents of the offspring. Waivers would be signed on cheap white paper with all sorts of consents and risk apparent signatures. Chaperones would be numerous and armed with plenty of threats and action to prevent any ill events. These students were newly minted adults and trust was needed of the group. "Trust me" was the mantra recited every day after school to the anxious parents who had yet to grant permission to anybody in this, as one said, "hare-brained scheme."

As the end of the year approached and weeks bore on, the idea matured as did the considerations of the parents. It was time for the Class of 1971 to be thrust the mantle of adulthood from society by their parents and anybody else that wanted to express congratulations. And handing it over, it would be. It would come to pass on a tropical island. Hundreds of miles into the Caribbean. On a ship. In the dark of night and in the light of day. Location unknown to man or beast, the sun somewhere buried on a horizon - untraceable on a cell phone, as there were none in existence. Chaperones would be symbolically leashed to each participant ensuring public safety and individual protection. The opportunity was too great to let pass. The adults had to admit that this was the prim de la prim of trips. A reward for these children of substance. The idea was good, but doubts remained buried deep in the cerebral cortex of sane adults, but these thoughts would be crushed for now, maybe retrieved later when the bus left.

The students could not speak of the idea without erupting into high pitched expression and waving of arms, about whether or not it would come to pass. Voices raised and lowered. The bottom line matured and suddenly no one believed it would ever transpire. No way. No how. Impossible. How could a multitude of hormone filled eighteen-year-olds be turned loose on the Commonwealth of the Bahamas?

They could endanger the entire country. Perhaps the world. A diplomatic incident could be awaiting, far more severe than the punishment Judge Horkan handed down in the simple "eggs on the mailboxes incident" that occurred one weekend in a school year. That was local and no property was destroyed, only made slimy and dirty. Nothing that a few penitent students couldn't remedy with soap and water, which they had done. Their sins were adjudicated with scrubbing and apologies. No harm. No foul. But with that incident, there were no international concerns or retributions from accent laced countrymen from another longitude and latitude.

One parent exclaimed, "Have you lost your mind?" "You can't even make curfew in this County." "You think that you deserve a trip to another civilization?" "On a boat, for God's sake!" Have you lost your mind in its entirety? What are you thinking? The majority of the students knew that it was time to get away from people who were asking them "What are you thinking?" There was the fear that some misdirected student might indeed tell his parents what he was contemplating.

The conversations were heated and loud in many homes at the end of each school day. The idea waxed and waned, mellowed and marched with early victories. City kids came in first, saying that "Mama was okay with it, but had to convince Daddy." There was a mild caste system of sorts in the school district. City kids vs country kids. It had always been that way. The ones living in the county came into Junior High after completing seven grades in the rural districts. Most were unknown to city students until the entrance into eighth grade accomplished by eighty passenger buses bringing the students into town. Rural bus riders, peering out the windows at the stained glass decorated churches of brick seemed to make the city kids closer to heaven than the ones in the country. The city folk would refer to "going uptown" while the country folk would "go to town." There were minor differences.

A story told by one man from the 1930's related that he and his county classmates were treated like immigrants from another country by the suave and smooth city dwellers. Looking back on it, he had to laugh as there wasn't much difference since the distance was less than ten miles, but it seemed a journey and a lifetime as a young child facing the city limits sign of Moultrie and the unknown.

Slowly over a four-week period many parents acknowledged that it might be possible. The country parents seemed to warm to the idea with influence from city parents. An iota of hope began to spring forth eternal in the psyche of the wide-eyed graduating seniors. It became possible, then likely, then probable. Then certain with money exchanging hands and documents signed.

Names of chaperones were put forth to allay the fears of the home front. The stature of the chaperones seemed to quieten the opposition. Noble people with good strong arms and minds. Successful law abiding Southerners. And most of all, the chaperones would be married couples, quick to discipline and mold the behavior. They could be entrusted with these somewhat adulted kids. Finally, some parents acknowledged defeat and acquiesced to the trip extraordinaire. The students that were permitted would be leaving the country for celebration on a cruise ship for graduation. A goodly number of around a hundred signed up, waivers were penned, money was saved and the student crowd of travelers watched the calendar. Other functions, like end of school gatherings and promenades took up the time and kept the adult's worries at bay for the last few months of the year.

Then suddenly life sped up and the high school graduation night was upon them. It loomed in the quick distance, weeks seemingly becoming minutes, then seconds. The days seemed to speed by like a Rock Island Rocket, a high-speed train, known only in Illinois. The earth had to be spinning faster on its axis. This could not be. The parents marveled that it had crept upon them like a quick night's rest, much like the passage of time with the entire 18 years of the student child.

Parents closed their eyes and opened them to find their offspring in the hats and gowns of graduation. Where had the time gone? How could life have whisked by as fast as a spilled Coke. Suddenly, first graders had entered elementary school in places like Funston, Hamilton, Reedy Creek, Stringfellow and Sunset. Then, time took off in a blur down an invisible runway. The parents marveled at the youth that stood before them. Dawn and dusk had merged together into a maze of life. They were all grown up, many having already outgrown the acne that so often plagued the early teenagers. Other still had enough hormonal aberration that mild cases remained much to the dismay of the students. All part of life and growing up. Nothing to be ashamed of or surprised at. Just an ordinary occurrence reflected by the mirror.

The parents also thought about the same question that would hit these children in their own thoughts and minds in the future. Fifty years from now, as adults, these offspring would realize that life had blown by like the proverbial sand from the hourglass. Like the "vapor" James talked about in his treatise. Marriages, divorces, births, deaths and other trauma will have come quickly in that fifty-year period.

But, at this point of graduation in 1971, all that future was ungrazed, unchartered and unfazed by the graduates. Only the immediate was mined. The shiny object so achieved. They stood. They adjusted hats and gowns. Hair was plastered to the head with gusto and some Vitalis. Shoes were shined. Make up was absorbed. A humid night in June became a petri dish for perspiration on upper lips, foreheads and underarms. The gowns were hot, but mandatory. Covered in the black cloth of graduation, students slid easily into the metal folding chairs lined up on the field. It was a weird feeling, sliding into an uneven folding chair. A sense of insecurity prevailed. Was it the shaky chair or the occasion that caused it?

They were nearing the end zone, at the goal post, ready to slide into a big fat touchdown of relief that pesky teachers would be sidelined, parental rules on suspension and restriction would have been decimated, or so they thought. Life would be theirs and theirs alone for conquering. Nobody needed any help this time. They were in charge and ready to show it and grab it with gusto and guts.

An aura of sadness a year earlier had laid across that graduation like a stifling fog that wouldn't break. It was unspoken. It hung like a thick sadness. Weeks before the event, a fine senior had drowned at Panama City Beach, Florida. A weekend trip had resulted in unspeakable tragedy. He already had a scholarship and a promise at a prestigious college. It never happened. Life intervened and then death. It seemed every year in high school brought tragedies to bare at the end of school. It was as if life was perfect, then a voice said, "No, it is not."

Tonight, all were ready. The only reluctance was the parents, who watched as the 18-year-olds, seemingly babies, preparing to take this leap into assumed stable citizens.

The group as a whole was a rock and roll generation. This was due initially to the Lads from Liverpool who had come to Atlanta Stadium five years earlier bringing their gyrating bodies, whacked off bowl haircuts and wearing what came to be called, "Beatle boots." The Monkeys followed. This resulted in that decade of many boys having been given hollow body Sears guitars for Christmas by their pleasing parents. Guitar lessons were taken at a small studio off the square in Moultrie. Some are still playing and singing fifty years later. The city kids were a little more upscale and had a few bands, electric guitars with larger amplifiers, loud drums, a keyboard and a bass guitar would complete the ensemble. Bookings were taken. A fun- filled psychedelic Volkswagen, envied by many, graced the streets with long haired citizens inside ready to break into a medley of rock and roll on any street corner, for any number of listeners. Numbers didn't matter, it was the aura, the ambiance, the friendship, the love among the graduates. It was the best of times for them all. This would be recognized years later as they turned in the night to face their memories from high school, so trite and ordinary then, now so bold and big and wistful to repeat "Take me back.", many would pause to think.

Tie dye shirts were in, starch was out. Vietnam raged and many registered students at the Selective Service were counted as 1 A- ready to go. They were nervous. The ones that went to college would be deferred. Some enlisted. Various antics had been done by students to avoid the draft. Rotten eggs were poured into ears prior to the physical in order to fail the physical. Two years earlier, Greg Alman, of The Alman Brothers had studied a picture of a foot skeleton, conjured up a "shooting party" with his brother Duane, and shot himself with a pistol between the first and second metatarsals. He showed up at the military office with crutches, a large bandage and was immediately deferred, as he had desired, in order to stay on tour with the band.

Students had hung out at The Bowl in Moultrie and heard bands like, The Tropics, B J Thomas, The Buckingham's, Ted Nugent and the Amboy Dukes, and Billy Jo Royal, a Georgia star whose claim to fame was "Down in the Boon Docs", a song immortalized by the "kicked down and out Southerners" as they were traversing the world. The students could identify with that song. It was sung frequently in the highways and byways of South Georgia.

The graduation line was long. The black and white high schools had merged a year earlier. A totality of students had fast become lifelong friends. The football team had improved immensely. Over four hundred names were called as womanhood and manhood marched on the turf of the field. Football and education go hand in hand in the South. Southern graduations are on the football field, almost a rite of holy passage, carefully monitored from the stands that held screaming fans on Friday nights all lit with excitement.

They walked across the stage, a rock and roll generation, molded by the assassination of the President in the fifth grade, by the War in Vietnam, by LBJ's Great Society and the Cuban Missile Crisis. They hoped for a future of perpetual love and long hair. Shags and mullets would be eternal.

There was love, the couples, the friends, the lives of youth from down the street, many from kindergarten forward. They had no way to know how long the love would last. Would love expire like a yellow banana from Hunnicutt's Grocery? Would it be all used up like some tube of Clearasil purchased at Watson's Drug Store? It would remain to be seen, but was not a concern at the moment, as far from the graduates as D Day in Normandy 25 years earlier. Wavering hair lines would stare back from mirrors in just a few years causing angst on the previously endowed students. The mullet and shag would thin.

The principal chimed in unison about the achievements and celebratory awards that were passed out. The main speaker, Congressman Dawson Mathis was a success story himself. Having served as an announcer at the local television station, he had catapulted himself into the Congress after a six-year stint in the living rooms of south Georgians delivering the news. It was a good success story and deserved to be told. He told it.

He was a consummate politician, tall, plenty of hair and popular mannerisms gleamed from his country boy upbringing in Berrien County, Georgia. He had just gone into the House of Representative on January 3, 1971. Six months later he was speaking at the high school graduation with great gusto. He became Chair of a House Agricultural Sub Committee and served 4 terms in Congress, losing a few years later when he gave up the house seat and ran for Senate. Sometimes you have to take a chance. He did and lost. He was unable to beat another winner, Senator Herman Talmadge. He disappeared from elective office and initiated Plan B, become a lobbyist.

But for now, he was wooing and encouraging squirming seniors in hot robes, high humidity and intolerable heat on a June night. He droned on but gave the students some good advice. Their minds were elsewhere. The closer to the ending, the movement seemed uncontrollable. Legs were crossed and stretched. Foreheads were wiped of perspiration on this night. Remarks were made as diplomas were handed out. It was not illegal yet, so the students sung Fairest Lord Jesus with vigor, strength and reverence. Nobody burned a flag, shouted at God or caused any adverse events. Prayer was prayed without ado. Heads bowed. Eyes closed. The Seniors were grateful to be alive in this beautiful time.

It was a pleasant moment. In those days, Jesus was a part of every public event. The world had not disavowed him yet. Nobody dreamed that Jesus would be kicked off the field in football games and graduations. But he was already sent home from the classroom.

The parents knew that certainly Jesus was satisficd with these graduates. The minds wandered. A trip loomed. Goodbyes were said and the crowd dispersed from the football field. Eighteen years had passed and the trek was over. Bedrooms would soon be empty as lives were begun in earnest and urgency.

The sky was dark in front of an antebellum home when a large number of graduated seniors mounted steps into a chartered bus. It was time. Vague light danced along the bus aisle, symbolic of a blurry unknown future that awaited their lives. Bumps and slamming were heard as suitcases were thrown into the side entry under the bus with force as if they were being tossed to a tropical island. A final boom

and the door had closed tightly. The driver leaped from the step into the seat as parents stared from the sidewalk in front of the residence. Much more smiling was apparent in the student group rather than those that were left to wonder how the trip would be and how the students would behave and return in one piece. As the students stared from darkened windows, the parents turned with backs to the bus, opened heavy car doors and drove away.

It was night time in South Georgia. The moon shone, beamed and reflected off the top of the bus. The bus lumbered out of town with a steady monstrous whine. The stars were out. Shadows of the pines greeted, then retreated. The group had passed from students to graduates in the mere blink of an eye. Algebra tests, French composition and music practice were fast removed. Fifty years later the memories would come more into focus than they were at that moment in that bus, but the gleeful graduates were unaware of that.

Time has a way of adjusting the focus in some sort of clarification that is not easily understood until we seem to look back and gain some better understanding from afar . Maturity.

The bus atmosphere was quieter than it should have been. It was the ripple of the moment, a realization that the landscape had been altered. The high school experience was over with an escapade looming ahead. The bus swayed and gently rocked sideways advancing down the road. It drove out of town past a Church of God known for a fiery preacher on Sunday mornings. Would pew holders squirm in his sermon next week? One thought it might depend on what we did this week. The thought vanished and Miami moved closer.

One became thirsty and availed himself of a large gulp of water from the bathroom sink at the back of the bus. He was unaware what "non-potable" meant. He was told by a smarter classmate that the water was not fit for drinking and that his intestines would decompose in minutes. This caused great anxiety but no one became sick. Who ever heard of available water coming from a sink that was unfit to consume? It was the first hint that maybe this group, contrary to what they thought, did not know all the intricacies of life. "Could life be unknown as of yet?", he wondered.

Miami seemed to lunge into view and arrived with it, the port. The ship, Bahama Star, was viewed with nervous laughter. One said it "looked bigger than he had imagined." Another said it "looked smaller."

Boarding commenced with great fanfare and marching of the students onto the deck seemed to make the ship drift from side to side. The ship then sailed into the sea, more bouncy and rugged than had been imagined, slicing bluntly through the water like a slim bullet creating a ditch in its wake with a bucking motion. The expanse of ocean in all directions seemed to greet a horizon in another universe. The size of the landscape of water was startling to most, calming to others. As in life, there were variances of thought even as the skyline seemed frozen.

There was some loud announcement in the air from an adult identified as our "Captain", who advised the ship rules of etiquette and a quasi-welcome that sounded a little tired, but maintained. It was hospitable and it was all the invitation that was needed. The Senior Cruise had begun whether the captain liked it or not.

A few hours later another announcement circulated that they were in international waters which to the more studious meant avoidance of behavior that could spike an international incident. The intent was not that however, it was advising the youth that water, alcohol or cokes could be drunk in abundance without identification or any proof of age or standing. No fake picture identification was required. One student had brought his own fake ID. It was quite unnecessary. As in real life, some availed of the liquids more than others who jumped headlong into the experience.

The glasses were round and tall with a hint of a pot belly middle section staring into the liquid. The shape would resemble some of the Seniors in a few years. The glasses carried décor including little umbrellas, stirrers, napkins and other paraphernalia that would make the experience more meaningful, if indeed, it could be remembered later at all. The drinks arrived with hence unknown names as if passwords to some distant land that needed a gatekeeper releasing the rewards to mortal man. Singapore Sling, Passion Hurricane, Pina Colada, Mai Tai and other words that had never been mentioned in a spelling bee by the Board of Education in Colquitt County and had never traversed the tongue of the graduates. Now, they were the vocabulary words of the day. Within minutes, the language of drinks rolled off the tongue with great familiarity, purpose and intent.

Arriving in Nassau, Bahamas the next morning, the harbor became visible and slowly enlarged into view. There was a sense of awe at this newly discovered terrain. The area adjacent contained a straw market and other tourist traps visible from the deck. There was no visible opulence.

It was learned that the students were free to leave the boat. No one would hold their hand and a departure time was given almost immediately. The idea of leaving the boat spread with astonishment to the students. Could this be? Somehow the former pupils would be disconnected from the captivity of the ship, its Captain and chaperones and be given free rein to explore Providence Island. A civilized mob of students left the boat on an unstable ramp as fast as humans could walk. The hot asphalt was hit by the masses. Streets like West Bay and Marlborough were discovered. Eye contact with Bahamians selling straw goods was avoided.

A student thought of his friend who had actually lived and worked in Nassau. He, with his father and another brother had built a hotel. The older son had carefully shipped his red Buick convertible to the island. The image of a boy from Reedy Creek, deep in the Caribbean, waving at Bahamian beauties from a red convertible on West Bay Street crossed his mind. A burst of laughter followed, unexplained to his passenger. It was true, he knew. A country boy will survive.

A motorcycle rental business was found and immediately a line formed. The cycles were Honda 50's, the tanks were full and they puttered off down the streets, paired up with lifelong friends on this new adventure. Absent was common sense. It was as if a grid search was being done on the island.

To onlookers it appeared that bikers were conducting search and rescue. They flew off leaving in all directions and at no slow rate of speed. The Bahama Star became a dot in the rearview mirror. The British, with its disjointed driving rules made it difficult for South Georgia drivers to traverse. Curves were scary on the Unamerican side of the road, but they were so happy that no thought was given to the realization that a wreck could happen. There was no trauma center for hundreds of miles and the Nassau Hospital likely had stale water and band aids. This was of no consequence. They were immune to misfortune. They were immortal, travelers in a new world with a life of freedom coming quickly.

Several immediately left and explored this new land from affluence to poverty in a New World of cultural unfamiliarity. Exploration did not mean observe and document. This was not the faun and fauna of Alexander the Great, to take a sample and report back. No. It meant stop and bond with Bahamian nature and beautiful beaches, wealthy neighborhoods with long stucco houses having gates and walls. It meant investigating the culture, knocking on doors and having tours of some of the homes. In one instance, far across the island, an eager homeowner took two students through the house and into the back yard.

A stucco swimming pool occupied half the back yard. As the owner clapped twice, a sea turtle the size of a small pony bobbed to the surface expecting a feeding. The named turtle was introduced to the students by the owner. Fifty the years later the name escapes. A friendly dolphin did an arc a few feet away. This was 1971. Perhaps now in 2024, the safety issue would be of concern. But this was a world of peace, love, and contentment that they were in at this time of their lives. They were immune to crime, mayhem and madness. They were in charge of the world. Nobody could take it away from them, even if the universe grabbed, it would come up shorthanded.

Miles and miles of territory was explored. Faces from pink and yellow stucco houses waved as if they were southerners, as the motorcycles sped by. The whole island was traversed. The day was over and it was back on the ship. Rumor was that only one broken bone in one party occurred on the jaunt.

As night fell, the ship knifed its way through the Caribbean. A few deck chairs were tossed overboard by partying students. It was more of a test of gravity and a physics question than an act of civil disobedience. Would the chairs float in an angry sea tossed to and for?   They did - and gently wafted off into the distance. The next logical question was asked. Would the chairs float with someone seated in them? Unknown. There were no takers for that experiment. The captain finally intervened with threats and promises of retribution as the students shaped up and ceased scientific inquiry.

Next, the life boats were discovered. Long, huge and bulky rowboat type craft were found to be assessable from the deck with a small amount of dangerous maneuvering, much like walking a gang plank. It was dark and questions of safety were considered but only for a millisecond, then trashed.

Would it be illegal to enter a lifeboat if no one was in danger? Probably. It would defeat the purpose of such lifeboat if no lives were in jeopardy. But did that matter? No. The question then rolled off the tongue, probably not asked since the Titanic, "Would you like to get into the lifeboat with me?"

A few steps on a dark plank and a small jump placed one directly into a life boat, apparently ready for immediate departure into the water below. A release lever was not found. It dangled and swayed.

To the graduates who found this experience, there was something mysterious and utterly awesome about gracefully relaxing and reclining in a lifeboat when you really don't have need for a lifeboat. It was like being in a horror story without being afraid. This could be the biggest mind fake out in the history of time. Folks in a life boat are generally in a state of hysteria, praying for survival and a rescue.

Think Titanic. When you are in a life boat as a disinterested party, it is death being cheated, robbed of its nature. You scream to the Caribbean, "You can't touch me, I am invincible.", as you dangle from a life boat. As lives were touched and thoughts shared, it was obvious that this was a unique event. Confessions in a life boat without fear of death. Bizarre. Like being in a foxhole at peacetime. What an aberration- a wrinkle of sorts with no trauma or bad ending.

However, all good things come to an end, and this episode was terminated by a huge spotlight held by the captain shining from 50 feet above and illuminating the lifeboats like a football field on Friday night. Occupants were ordered out and dispersed as requested. No names were taken and the graduates disappeared into the crowd with a story for fifty years later.

It was then discovered that fire extinguishers will function appropriately without the presence of flames, heat or fire. Much to the near hysteria of the cabin dwellers, a young, calm, man shot one with its thick white foam into various rooms. He ran for his life and was not caught or disciplined. He was last seen running down a narrow corridor at record speed swinging a fire extinguisher as he leaped around the corners with a high-pitched laughing scream filling the air somewhere between hysterical and psychotic. A cabin boy, viewing himself as the patrol of the galley, made a futile run to capture the perpetrator.

This was unsuccessful. The runner disappeared into the wind.

Suddenly, the days and nights disappeared and the cruise ended as quickly has it had begun. The bus in the Miami Port was boarded and a quiet, sunburned, group, appearing dazed, but unconfused, returned to South Georgia.

The trip was a topping, like an accessory of sorts, planted on the hopes and dreams of the graduates. They would never forget it nor regret it. It was there to stay. Deep, pleasant memories of a great time had across the sea by boat. It was the first adventure within hours of graduating high school.

Upon returning home, one set of parents had undergone an epiphany of sorts. Prior to the trip, this couple had purchased the graduate a red 1971 Cutlass Convertible. It was driven right off the lot of Gene Hodges Chevrolet. The salesman, a fine lover of youth, had somehow captured the parent's deepest desires to provide this set of hot wheels to the son. But, alas, the garage was empty when he returned home.

The story emerged. The mother, driving the convertible, was treated to a few words relating to the song, "Little Ole Lady from Pasadena." Wild students screamed the lyrics as they blew by in an old Chevrolet hardtop. Probably intimidated, the incident, combined with thoughts of the cost of college, caused the parents to return the car to the dealer. The salesman was gracious enough to take it back and allay the souls of the parents. The boy was disappointed, but was not surprised. It all seemed a dream anyway, and he was still on an emotional high from gallivanting around the Bahamas like Columbus discovering America.

By fifty years after the Senior Trip, graduates realized that they had grown up. It had taken years, but the mystery was revealed and the blurry became focused. Disappointingly, they realized that it was not when a bespectacled aunt had pinched cheeks at a reunion when they were 12, and recited, "You have grown up." It was not then. It was not, when Burt Reynolds said that it was "when your daddy says you have." The maturation came in multiple ways, at a time of grief over a loss, or joy over a birth. Growing up meant getting older and sensing that the world can bring events of good and bad of which we are a part. Some good. Some bad. As Mark Twain said, "I was amazed when I returned home to realize how much my parents had learned and grown while I was gone." He didn't realize that the change was in him, not the parents.

Eventually the realization hits. It may take years. But when it happens, it seems natural and without doubt. Stone cold, sober, real thoughts hit like a log truck. Boom. Crunch. Suddenly, the graduates realized that they were full grown in season, like the gathered tobacco on sticks in the barn, slow cooking for the market, then drying and gracing the warehouses in South Georgia.

It was much like putting on new glasses at age 10 in Dr. Paulk's office. The mother, expressing doubt that one would wear them was reassured that the boy would not want to take them off. Seeing, for the first time, that trees had leaves resulted in the use of habitual glasses. The boy asked, "Would dreams at night be clearer if glasses were worn when he slept?"

Maturity. Focus. Thoughts. Births. Deaths. Joys. Disappointments. Achievements. Growing up means a few simple things, but it has to be the metamorphosis, the merging, the blending, the consummate binding that earth life does. There are soft spots formed and rugged areas for protection. All healed up

-scarred, thick and tender at the same time. Maturity, like a big old oak. Always weathered, never on the ground, containing limbs to climb and hug, and providing protection overlying the young sprouts coming up from below.

Some grasp eternal truth, the ultimate, that God is over all. Faith. Some steady, some Jello seeming with tremors. They've been hurt. Broken. Others somehow avoid upsets and setbacks and settle quite peacefully into living life. Stoic. Untorn. Always upbeat. You wonder, have they ever had a bad day? Everything seems to be a habit, a custom or a routine. Others thrive on the unorthodox living in a state of perpetual surprise. Impulsive. Urgent. Screaming at the world and expecting a response.

Everyone is different, yet the maturation is the same. We all grow up. Grandmother can hold the tops of the heads but the growth does not stop. The heads will pass her and be looking down upon her in seemingly seconds.

That as it might be, the graduation was a period or maybe a pause or comma at the end of a sentence depicting birth, parents, school, activities and studies. This segment of life was lived, one strand having been accomplished. They were finally old enough to look back, though in the scheme of things, it was a short look, birth to 18 years, but none the less, they could now pontificate about living.

The future was always around the corner but now it had leaped out, no longer unattainable. We knew the future would continue to advance and we knew that we would be a part of it. Bedrooms at the homeplace would be empty as the graduates embarked on their own life. Parents would spend sleepless nights concerned with their offspring, as the children wondered how life would be without parental oversight.

The years passed and the thoughts, struggles, accomplishments and fears have been moved along to us, the Class of 1971. As we prepare to do the handoff to the next generation, we can agree that the years have had ups and downs with a whole lot of blessings interspersed. Most of us, I ponder, would not want to start over. Through God's grace, we are here. We made it and life is good.

ABOUT THE AUTHOR

Dr Ted Ary grew up in Moultrie, Georgia, attended Harding University, Illinois College of Podiatric Medicine and a hospital program at Doctors Hospital, Tucker, Georgia. He practiced Podiatric Medicine and Surgery for forty years in South Georgia before retiring.

He enjoys spending time with his wife, Cindy, daughters, and grandchildren. He loves writing, enjoys the beach and mountains, spending time in both.

Made in the USA
Columbia, SC
02 June 2025